Sis and Sid

by Isabelle Minturn
illustrated by David Austin Clar
Practice Decodable 11

Mc Graw Hill Education

Bothell, WA • Chicago, IL • Columbus, OH • New York, NY

MHEonline.com

Send all inquiries to:
McGraw-Hill Education
8787 Orion Place
Columbus, OH 43240

ISBN: 978-0-02-146206-3
MHID: 0-02-146206-2

Printed in China.

8 9 10 11 12 DSS 27 26 25 24 23

Sid sits and sits.

Did Sis sit?

Sid sits on sand.

Did Sid see it?

It is up, Sid!

Sid did see it!